Braille for Babies

© CREATIVE EDUCATION

Prologue

This book is the perfect guide for beginners in understanding the fundamentals of Braille. The book introduces you to the alphabet and numbers in Braille. It contains activities to hone your basic Braille skills.

The book has been created in an un-indented format, to facilitate reading of the Braille text. A stylus/embosser can be used to indent the illustrations for an enhanced effect.

- Creative Education

History of Braille

Braille, universally accepted system of writing used by and for <u>blind</u> persons and consisting of a <u>code</u> of 63 characters, each made up of one to six raised dots arranged in a six-position matrix or cell. These Braille characters are embossed in lines on paper and read by passing the fingers lightly over the manuscript.

The writing system for the blind known as Braille was invented by the French student Louis Braille in 1824. At the time, he was 15 years old and attending France's Royal Institute for Blind Youth.

The school had a number of books in which the letters were raised, but these were hard to both make and read. After hearing about a military code using raised dots, he created a simpler system to represent French regular and accented letters. He first published a description of his system, including musical notation, in 1829.

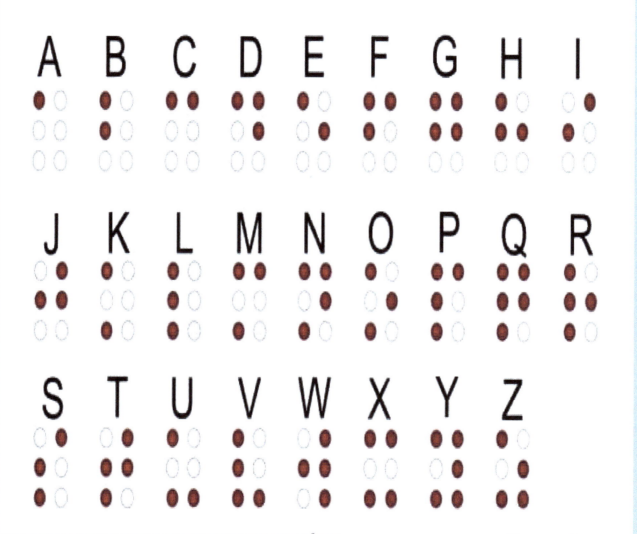

The Braille Alphabet

a b c d e f g h i

k l m n o p q r s

u v w x y z

but	can	do	every	from	go
have	just	knowledge	like	more	not
people	quite	rather	so	that	us
very	will	it	you	as	

I love you very much

Draw a line to connect the print letters to the correct braille letter.

and	
to	
child	
still	
the	
with	
of	

My Name in Braille

My Name in Braille

Practise writing your name in Braille

Write the words below in braille

Theme "Back To School"

teacher	
class	
learn	
school	
friends	

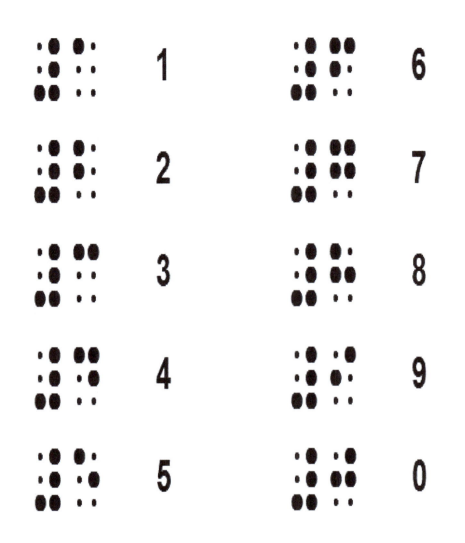

Numbers in Braille

Char	Unicode Name	Braille
=	Equals sign	⠀⠀
←	Leftwards arrow	⠀⠀⠀⠀
↑	Upwards arrow	⠀⠀⠀⠀
→	Rightwards arrow	⠀⠀⠀⠀
↓	Downwards arrow	⠀⠀⠀⠀
∀	For all	⠀⠀
∂	Partial differential	⠀⠀
∃	There exists	⠀⠀
∈	Element of	⠀⠀
∉	Not an element of	⠀⠀⠀
∑	N-ary summation	⠀⠀⠀
∞	Infinity	⠀⠀
∩	Intersection	⠀⠀
∪	Union	⠀⠀
∫	Integral	⠀
≃	Asymptotically equal to	⠀⠀⠀
≠	Not equal to	⠀⠀⠀
≡	Identical to	⠀⠀
≤	Less-than or equal to	⠀⠀⠀
≪	Much less-than	⠀⠀⠀⠀⠀
⟨	Mathematical left angle bracket	⠀⠀⠀
∫∫∫∫	Quadruple integral operator	⠀⠀⠀⠀

⠐⠣⠭⠐⠤⠼⠛⠐⠜⠐⠣⠼⠉⠚⠐⠨⠌⠼⠑⠐⠜⠀⠐⠶⠀⠼⠁⠓

(x - 7)(30 ÷ 5) = 18

⠼⠋⠭⠐⠤⠼⠙⠃⠀⠐⠶⠀⠼⠁⠓

⠼⠋⠭⠀⠐⠶⠀⠼⠋⠚

⠭⠀⠐⠶⠀⠼⠋⠚⠐⠌⠋

⠭⠀⠐⠶⠀⠼⠁⠚

Try some sums in braille

You can do it !

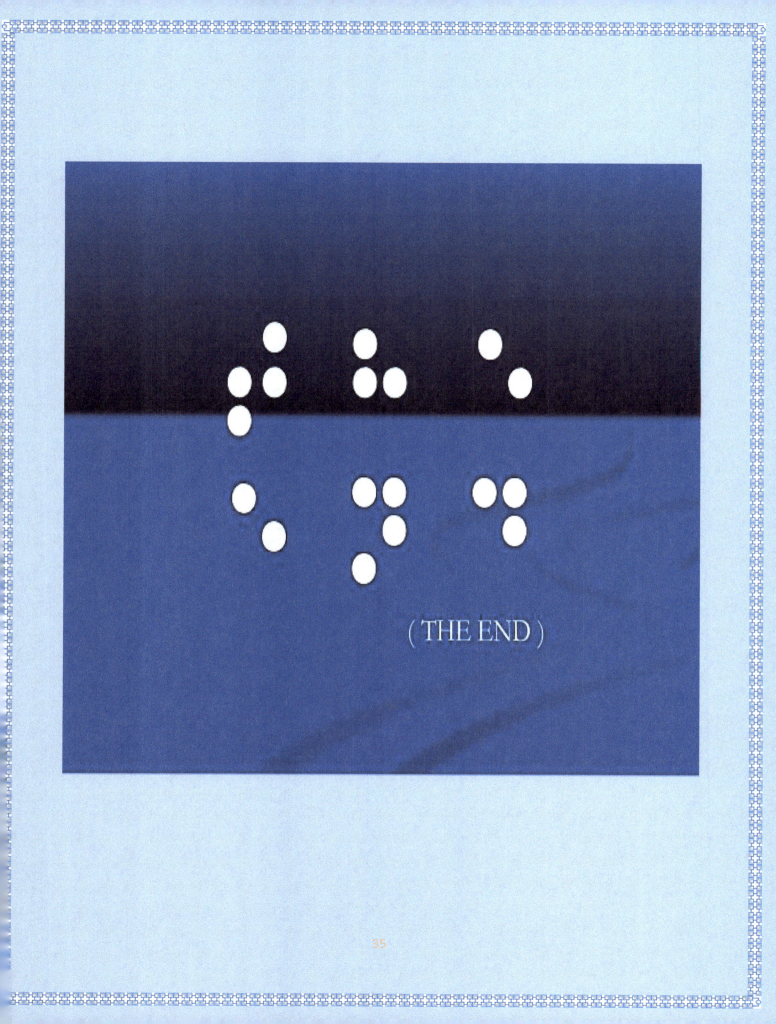

(THE END)

WHO INVENTED BRAILLE?

Louis Braille

4 January 1809 – 6 January 1852)

He was a French educator and the inventor of a reading and writing system named after him, <u>braille</u>, intended for use by <u>visually impaired</u> people.

His system is used worldwide and remains virtually unchanged to this day.

Braille was blinded at the age of three in one eye as a result of an accident with
a <u>stitching awl</u> in his father's <u>harness</u> making shop.

Consequently, an infection set in and spread to both eyes, resulting in total blindness.

At that time, there were not many resources in place for the blind, but he nevertheless excelled

in his education and received a scholarship to France's <u>Royal Institute for Blind Youth</u>.

While still a student there, he began use of a <u>tactile</u> code that could allow blind people to read and write quickly and efficiently.

Inspired by a system invented by <u>Charles Barbier</u>, Braille's new method was more compact and lent itself to a range of uses, including music.

He presented his work to his peers for the first time in 1824, when he was fifteen years old.

In adulthood, Braille served as a professor at the Institute and had a vocation as a musician, but he largely spent the remainder of his life refining and extending his system.

It went unused by most educators for many years after his death.

However, posterity has recognized braille as a revolutionary invention, and it has been adapted for use in languages worldwide.

SOME EQUPMENT USED TO WRITE IN BRAILLE

STYLUS

REGLET

BRAILLER

References   [Accessed on 29.12.20]

Home | American Foundation for the Blind (afb.org)

Modern Usage of Braille in Today's Society - Vocalink Global

(PDF) Transliteration of Digital Gujarati Mathematical Text into Braille for Visually Impaired People (researchgate.net)

Follow The Leader: Brownie "Senses" Badge (followthejrleader.blogspot.com)

Braille Transcription Services - Braille Works

What is Braille? | Lighthouse for the Visually Impaired and Blind (lvib.org)

5 Interesting Facts for World Braille Day: January 4, 2016 (brailleworks.com)

Braille | writing system | Britannica

Braille - History of Braille (softschools.com)

LOUIS BRAILLE (ENGLISH) (slideshare.net)

Braillealphabet.org

Louis Braille - Wikipedia

Braille Practice Worksheets - Practice Worksheets (noveltodays.com)

Books by Creative Education

BABY LOVES ALPHABETS

BABY LOVES NUMBERS

BABY LOVES SHAPES

BABY LOVES COLOURS

BRAILLE FOR BABIES

BABY LOVES SIGNS

www.ingramcontent.com/pod-product-compliance
Lightning Source LLC
LaVergne TN
LVHW080727121224
798946LV00006B/632